WELCOME TO MY WORLD

A book of poems for infinity

By Joshua Muñoz
LOVER BOY IN SPACE

#loverboyinspace

3rd Edition (2025)

WELCOME TO MY WORLD – A book of poems for infinity
Copyright © 2023 Joshua Muñoz

Cover by author.

Independently published in the United States by Joshua Muñoz

All rights reserved. No part of this publication may be reproduced in any form, or by any means, electronic or mechanical, including photocopying, recording, or any information browsing, storage, or retrieval system, without permission in writing from the publisher. For information, contact the publisher: jmunoz0521@gmail.com

ISBN 9798852549150

www.loverboyinspace.medium.com

This is a work of fiction. Unless otherwise indicated, all the names, characters, businesses, places, events and incidents in this book are either the product of the author's imagination or used in a fictitious manner. Any resemblance to actual events is purely coincidental.

Dedicated to everyone I love, us and infinity

TABLE OF CONTENTS

CHAPTER 0. I'VE BEEN WAITING

CHAPTER 1. GROW UP. 1

- 2 TO THE MOON
- 5 REPEAT
- 6 YOU DIVINE DISEASE
- 7 THE GIRL IN MY DREAMS
- 9 FIRECRACKER
- 10 SOMEWHERE FAR, THE MORNING CREEPS
- 12 I FORGOT
- 14 MY LITTLE GHOST
- 15 IMY
- 16 I SPY
- 17 ANGER AND ENVY
- 19 BURN
- 20 SPACE DUST
- 21 SORRY
- 23 SHINY RINGS
- 25 RUN, MOON BOY, RUN

CHAPTER 2. MOON BOY. 26

- 27 COLORBLIND CHAMELEON
- 28 WEIRDO
- 30 FRESHMAN
- 32 THE ESCAPE ARTIST
- 33 PRETTY
- 34 SPLATTERED PAINT
- 35 OH, BOTHER.

36 SEROTONIN DEALER
37 MUDDY SHOES
38 SUNBURNT MEMORIES
39 JUMPING OUT OF PLANES

CHAPTER 3. COLOR.
41

42 GRAYISH GRAY
44 SPACE-LOOT
45 PENTHOUSE POOL DISCO
46 BLUE FRUIT
47 SUN BATH
48 ORANGE JELL-O
49 PLUM SPRINKLES
50 LUNCH DREAM
53 POCKET MONSTERS
54 LEAKY GOGGLES
55 ZOMBIELAND
56 I WANT TO LIVE IN THE TV
57 GROOVY BABY
58 YOU ARE THE COLOR OF LIFE TO MY CORNEA
59 PSYCHEDELIC COMET
60 TWENTY-EIGHT MINUTES LEFT ON THE ROAD, WEDNESDAY
61 POLAR SNOW-ANGEL
62 THE FOREST OF TOMORROW ENVELOPES THE ATOMS OF OUR SOULS

CHAPTER 4. LOVE LETTERS FROM SPACE.
63

64 THE SEA AND THE SUN.
65 PROTOSTAR
67 GROWN UP
69 EUROPA ON THE SOFA

70 HOOKED
71 HER SOUNDTRACK
73 LOVE DRUNK
74 DIVINE CHEMISTRY
75 HIGH TIDE
76 LATE NIGHTS, LAUGHING WITH YOU
78 LAUNDROMAT ON CESAR CHAVEZ
79 QUEEN TACO
80 PLAYER 2
81 YOU'RE A SALAD.
82 LA LOTERÍA
83 A SUNDAY AFTERNOON WITH MARISOL
84 WHAT'S YOUR FAVORITE ACTIVITY WHEN NOT BEING PERFECT?
85 HEY SLEEPING BEAUTY
86 MARISÓL

CHAPTER 5. VOLUME.
87

88 THIS IS FINE.
89 CLAUSTROPHOBIC ASTRONAUT
91 HEY, IT'S ME AGAIN.
92 BREIGH-BORLY PEOPLE
93 WORKING ON SATURDAY
94 NARRATORS:
95 EXERCISE
96 LOVER BOY IN SPACE
97 MAKE IT STOP!
98 EMOTE
99 THIS IS NOT FINE.
100 SYSTEM CRASH
101 6:37PM
102 TOP-LOAD HEAVY
103 HOW LONG CAN I TALK ABOUT MYSELF?
104 QUARTZ
105 BRB.

106   DILUTED SUN AND MOON GOLD PAVEMENT
107   TORCHED
108   NEGATIVE NINETY-TWO
109   I WALK IN THE LAND OF BUTS
110   DETACH
111   I'M SENDING BESOS FOR YOUR BRAIN.
112   SUN ROSE
113   KANGAROOS SLAM UP NORTH
112   THE ORBIT
113   LA NIÑA NOCHE

CHAPTER 6. NIGHT. 116

117   BLACK-RABBIT HOLE
118   DRUNK IN THE BATHROOM
119   CORRUPTED FILES
121   LIQUID COURAGE
123   UNDER THE INFLUENCE
126   UPSIDE DOWN
128   SNOOZE YOUR POCKET WATCH
129   SUMMER SHEETS HOLD THE SUN AND SEAS
130   TACOS ARE DANCING SALSA IN MY ATTIC.
131   GPS SIGNAL LOST.
132   LORENA & WHITTIER
133   KETO SHAKESPEARE
134   TELESCOPIC
135   SLEEPY

CHAPTER 7. SELF PORTRAIT. 136

137   SELF PORTRAIT-JOSHUA MUNOZ.32

CHAPTER 0. I'VE BEEN WAITING

WELCOME TO MY WORLD

Iridescent skylines
twisted
behind lime-capped, pastel mountains
as far as the eye can see —
Roads, erratic, always under construction

We go skinny dipping in mental hurricanes,
all year round, all whilst a bright,
warm star
spins
in
and out of view,
dancing with my ever-changing mood;
Sodium-chloride and vodka torrents
sometimes flood river banks when I'm blue

On good days,
unfettered sunflowers
bob atop atmospheric
swells
like
cocoa butter-scented snowflakes
floating
in
low
gravity

Chromatic deserts of dry paint
straggle throughout my world map,
possessed
by ancient voices
wispering into the chalky winds
You don't belong here . . .

There's also volcanic eruptions
and panic-inducing nuclear blasts
which
radiate the most gorgeous, blue and violet
autumn-noon
sunsets

Pardon
the space dust,
 as we figure this shit out

CHAPTER 1. GROW UP.

Younger lover boy.

TO THE MOON

Today, I'm leaving, saying goodbye.
I'll be back soon, so please don't cry.
I've made up my mind — just look at my face.
This kid is flying to outer space!

A few sad waves are shared before the trip,
then it's time to start this sweet spaceship.
Mission control says all is clear.
I push the switch—*I'm out of here!*
My homemade rocket's become a blur, shooting
past where people were.

Higher, higher, and higher I go,
my big blue world is
shrinking
below.

Soon, I soar in a sea of stars,
think I almost see the dusts of Mars.
My eyes widen as I look around.
I want to stop, but I can't slow down.
With butterflies inside of me,
I continue looking out into
infinity.

The things I see I can barely describe.
I watch them all float and wizz on by—
beautiful colors and shapes, with massive
galaxies swimming in heaven's lake.
Lost in space, my fears are gone, as my little ship
glides along.

I've got my face pressed against the window,
when flashing lights announce I'm near.
The moon's in sight, I'm finally here!

As I approach, the rocket slows—
closer and closer, I drop and float.
A mighty cloud erupts as my ship hits land,
leaving my window covered by swirling sands.
I unlock the latch, lift up and look down.
Without a pause, I push off and jump out.

Like a child's toy lost in the ocean,

my body hangs in space,

and floats down in slow motion.

Time seems to stop as I descend.

Past, present, future, all start to blend.

So calm and at peace, this feeling is new.

I stare out into space and see the world I knew.

I finally made it.

I'm all alone.

Far from you, and far from home.

No pictures of how we used to be.

No radio playing our songs on repeat.

Light-years away,

I've found a place the memories may soon erase.

I smile, the first smile in so long.

I believe I can finally move on.

Soft as a feather, my body falls flat.
I close my eyes to rest,
when your face stares back . . .
I flinch and sigh—so much for that.
All the way to my moon I flew,
as far as I could, but you came too.

REPEAT

Though you hold me tight,
this moment of ours is fleeing.
This you and me we're seeing,
this love and all its warmth your feeling,
will soon be gone.

It happens every time.
And it's coming soon, I know it—
that dreadful moment when it all falls apart.
I'm crying, baby, why aren't you?
Aren't you terrified of this part too?
Can't you see the future,
all the changes we're going to go through?

With time, this love will disappear.
Every happy moment and kiss we shared,
forgotten, ripped away . . . like they always do.

But I so badly want us to be different;
forever's how long I want this feeling to stay.
I wish, like our favorite songs, that we'd never change.

Baby, please, break the hour glass for me.
Play this moment on a loop and press repeat.
Look into my eyes,
lost in love with me for eternity—
I don't ever want to lose you.
I don't ever want to lose you.
I don't ever want to lose you.
I don't ever want to lose you.

YOU DIVINE DISEASE

I wish
I infested your brain like you do mine
You virus, cancer—
benign, "so nice"
How thoughtful to stay
and widen your grip

You drug, pill,
schedule-one narcotic—
you think you're so freakin' dope
Bloodshot eyes you give me
With heroin blood, I'm spinning . . .
I'm addicted and your needle
is lost in my veins

You divine disease.
I wish I infected you—
tainted,
corrupted, corroded,
every corner of your body—
like you so selfishly do me

I wish, but reality and wishes
are very different

THE GIRL IN MY DREAMS

Sometimes, I wonder, why do you leave?
You're unlike other girls, I only see you when I sleep.

When I wake,
do you know I feel crazy
for expecting you next to me?

Every morning,
you leave my poor heart mourning
when an empty spot in my bed
is all that's lwft where you had slept.

You were here when I was sleeping
— where did you go?
I see your face when I'm dreaming
— your name, I won't know.

It might b3 the booze to tell you the truth.
Nights when I'm alone, the bottle goes dawn smooth.
And as these elixirs
disappear in the abyss here in my room,
I find myself again in the company of you.

Maybe I need one of those
therapists to help explain this —
you're not real, but in my dreams, my dear,
you exist.

You've becpme an invisible drug.
You're like my night-time lucid liquor
—my siesta tequila*!*

Your presence in my dreams hath me
perpetually drunk with your illusion of love.

But yeah . . .
This bottle's getting a bit low —
 and I'm not surw if I still make sense right now.

How about we just disr3gard these slurred words?
I'm gonna hit the lights
and knock out n0w.

See yoi soon.

FIRECRACKER

Adiós,
goodbye,
you temporary high.
Thanks for the laughs, for the joy and the lust.

For the bright hope of love
you brazenly teased, thank you
for that too.

While it lasted, it was dazzling,
but then. . . you know. . .
FLASH! CRACK! POP!

— you blew it up.

What a shame.
I wish you the best, I guess.
I don't know what else to say.
I really hope you felt the same way
that I did,
and you regret your decision every day.

Long after time's erased
our little firecracker flame from my brain,
I hope I haunt you.

Yes, decades later,
when your lover lies under the blankets
you share, I hope deep down
you worry
that he will never compare.
That, secretly, you wish I was there.

I hope you doubt that man you love,
And, while he sleeps so peacefully,
you look at him and wonder.
Just how happy could you have been,
if he
were me?

SOMEWHERE FAR, THE MORNING CREEPS

My weary eyes, do you deceive?
Is it thee—could it be?
Who knows how I found you here.
I don't know why, and I don't care.
I missed you, babe,
and you missed me too.
To have you back's a dream come true.

Let's talk and talk, and keep on laughing.
We'll joke around like nothing happened.

I can't remember the reasons why
we walked away or said goodbye.
It all seems so far away, far away we let it lay.
Hours pass, time flies by.
You swear this time you are forever mine.

But oh, my love, woe is me,
somewhere far,
 the morning creeps.

This world we reside won't last for long.
I'll hold you close, but you'll still be gone.

See, soon, the sun will rise and shine.
The world will wake,
and so shall I.

Helpless, I'll watch you fade,
be forced to wave farewell
to you and this cursed place.

The morning light will flood my eyes;
a new dreaded day begins, another
damned dream
dies.

You're still with him,
and I'm in bed—

a broken boy
alone again.

I FORGOT

I forgot about love.

I forgot about all of it.

I forgot about the feeling
of "missing" someone.
I forgot their face all day
plastered on your brain.
I forgot about "being together"
being never too soon,
and "time to go" coming all too quick.
I forgot about "just ten more minutes"
  — never satisfied.

I forgot play fights.
I forgot about kisses that stop time.
I forgot about "I love you"—
those words a drug, the purest high.

I forgot about real fights.
I forgot about anger.
I forgot about cruel words you know aren't true.
About silence, pride and cold shoulders,
when inside you're dying, praying
the other breaks.

I forgot about "I'm sorry".
I forgot about forgiveness
and kisses that clear tears away.

I forgot about romance.
I forgot about carefully chosen cards
with pages crammed in ballpoint ink.
I forgot about counting pennies
for blossoms to give — just because.

I forgot about "the quiet".
When the world is loud
and your worries louder,
but, somehow, they all fade away —
like magic, they vanish
every time you're around her.

I forgot about love,
 and it hurts to remember.

MY LITTLE GHOST

There is a ghost that follows me around.
Always by my side, it never makes a sound.
It's been there awhile now,
I can't recall how long, though.

Nowadays,
 I go about not noticing it follow.

Sometimes it makes me smile, and
sometimes it can hurt.
Nobody sees the bruises, nor ever will, I'm sure.

Throughout the day, it climbs
and clambers up my back.
At night, it nestles close, whispers 'til I'm sad.

An endless cycle, I rise and repeat.
I don't believe I'll ever be free.

Perhaps, I'll wake one day
alone
in my sheets—
when I look in the mirror, it'll just be me . . .

Until then, though,
it reflects that heartbreaking face.
"Come on, little ghost, it's time for the day."

IMY

I hate you
More than a hangover at work.

I entrusted you my heart, your
Soft little hands were once its shelter from pain.
Shame on you to make me so happy.
You were the sugar in my coffee, the
Oil in my engine, the sunlight in my storm, yet
Unremorsefully, you broke me and went on your way.

Spoiled milk truly tastes better than your name.
Offered a choice between hell or a day back with you,
My pick might change my zip code — 02666.

Unquestionably, this will be my last goodbye.
Crackling flames now hold every last memory of ours—
Hope your cold heart burns like our photographs on fire.

I SPY

Do you see the things I do?
The hidden web, you see it too?
Each step I take connects a dot.
Her face I see where she is not.
Insane, I've gone?
Mad, am I?
 Or, do you spy the things I spy?

Unseen, tangled-up ties, the links to before,
a phrase in a flick,
a scent that she wore.

All around, every second, I'm tormented
by cleverly concealed connections to my past.
Walking through cities of dreams,
it's becoming hard to tell if I'm
awake
or
asleep.

Every night, in my dark room, her face
glows bright, as radio
ballads bring her sad spirit to life.
Do you see her, dancing for me—
her smile and eyes so mesmerizing?

Sigh . . .
Mad, sad, I've lost my mind,
crumbled away by love and time.
Can't you see the things I see? Take them
from me,
won't you please?

ANGER AND ENVY

Oh, grumpy little boy in the mirror,
what happened to you?
What empty muse has cut short
your long fuse?

       I'M ANGRY AT YOU, DAMN IT
       I'm angry at life and every damn
       person
       who conveniently finds what I've
       searched IN VAIN
       so desperately for

My heart
held a home for hope once
Now, love's broken roots
have grown rage in replace

I hate that I'm the broken one and not them
Somehow, in love, I've ended up useless—
like a once shiny bike now beat-up and old,
deflated tires and twisted spokes
wobbling persistently
and painfully
in the dark

"There's so many fish in the sea," they say,
as they surf with their lovers
to happily ever after.
But how the fuck do I find "the one"
out of these multiplying billions
taunting my heart with potential?
All just to end up like last week's
tuna salad —
unwanted, forgotten

All I ever wanted was
a home for this humble love of mine
Some safe, quiet place to shed this dead
skin, try and grow new again —
but such a fate would be too generous for me,
apparently

NO VACANCY mocks my tired feet
at every corner like some vile conspiracy
to make a fool of the gullible, dumbass kid
still reading fairy tale stories, believing
a soulmate is really out there somewhere
—some specially-created "perfect partner"
just waiting cheerfully
and patiently for him

Who decided these OBNOXIOUS
and selfish people—flaunting their priceless
treasure recklessly—deserve love and happiness
more than I do?
Bullshit, fuck them all . . .

All this struggle for uninsured prizes
We lie and we tell ourself
"today's the day" every day,
and we know deep down
how stupid we sound, yet still
we fucking
say it

We believe it,
like the idiot we are
And the world cheers and laughs,
as we, the dim-headed dreamer, continue
day after day after day after day
in this f ucking NEVER-ENDING game
—so, sorry if I'm a little fucking
angry
OK?

ok.

BURN

In my hands, I hold a fire
It used to be wild,
an uncontrollable sea
of scorching waves,
and *you* — you used to be the fuel

But then, one day.
you left, remember?

For years since then,
I've held these embers
of our beautiful disaster
— my hope to rekindle the inferno
Your spirit has always lingered
in the soft glow
nearby, a constant reminder of warmth
just out of reach

However, it's time for you to burn now
Together, we are chaos,
lava and lightning,
a glorious union not meant to be
After too many years, I can finally see

A FLARE ERUPTS, and here I am,
face to face with you again

Head to toe you are set ablaze,
staring at me silent
Empty eyes of an empty shell,
you left me cold in a living hell
Burn, burn, burn, and please never return

SPACE DUST

Be honest. Quit with your cowardice and fraud.
Say what you need to say, and let the universe play on.
You narcissistic, pathetic fucking bum.
Invertebrate,
parasite whom love, deserveth not,
admit you're full of empty words
and feces. That you flee at first sign
from the mortifying expectations
and responsibilities of the real world
because you're a scared vain-little-bitch.

Keep playing pretend
in your head
—NO, YOU'RE NOT A BAD GUY, JOSHUA.

Go indulge in your shallow solitude–
waste away and avoid reality
cottling your paper-thin ego
until the Earth is nothing but asteroids
drifting out to speckled black sea,
floating irrelevantly through the waves of space
and time
with your
 infinitely worthless dust.

SORRY

How'd it happen?
How did your innocent Prince Charming
change so drastically?
So sweet when the story started
 —now look at him.
Little devil.
Fake angel dressed in white clothing.
Horns on his head,
fake halo and everything. Shit,
I bet you think you know
who this scumbag asshole really is.
This romantic gentleman
weaving sugar-laced words that rope you in.
Admit it, you fell for it.
He told you he was different,
and you believed it.
Now, your knight in shining white armor's
become the one you feared.
Nothing but a self-righteous beast
lurks beneath his helmet
—now you see it clear.
And you look so disgusted.
Sick of all the honey sweet talk
dripping out your ear.
Sick of endless games played
that end up nowhere.
The cat's out the bag,
it isn't cute anymore.
I can see it in your face,
you can't do this anymore.
I can see it in your damp irises, you finally realize
who made a fool of you
   —who pulled the wool right over your eyes...

It was *me*
you let in,
and you'll hate yourself forever for it.
Though you don't deserve it,
your broken heart
will forever have a piece stuck in my teeth.

I had good intentions, darling,
I apologize —
I really tried —
but in the end a wolf's
still a wolf,
even in sheep's disguise.

SHINY RINGS

Love, you would think,
is a simple concept
—but I, myself, can't quite seem to find it.

The thing is
I want better than average, so I wait.
I want better than okay, good, or great even.
I want someone real, not one fake feeling.

I ask that she's caring and humble.
I don't want her to be consumed
with what other people think or do;
let them judge, let them hate,
let them all live freely as they choose.

I want to be appreciated by her.
I want to know that she notices.
You know those little things,
done with love in mind, that time seems to shrink
in value so easily.

Goodnight texts can be golden, you know?
Doing dishes never gets old, and
I just think it'd be pretty cool to feel valued
for making those cold and flu medicine
trips
when she gets sick.

I want to be loved, so I hope
she's loving. Like some classic
poker,
hope she's all in, no limits
to her love-giving abilities.
Even on angry nights,
I hope she finds the will to still love me.

I imagine her kisses can take me to the moon;
I want her lips to be all mine.
My own private spaceship
to fly me away
when this world gets rough.

I hope she craves my affection
like pregnant girls and pickles,
or hot fudge sundaes on hot Sundays.

I want someone with a spirit
untamed,
young at heart but mature in mind,
excited for life.

She'll be a bright light glowing,
 her soul beautiful in a gloomy world.

And, I know what I want might be
just some naïve, selfish dream. So,
above all, I want to love her
the way she deserves to be loved.
Hold her so close, so she'll never forget
just how
ocean trench deep
I'm drowning in love.

I want that shiny ring, where angels sing—
never give her up, real sprung type feeling.
I pray I'm everything she's ever waited for.

I hope the love is so simple, it's scary, but
when the time comes, I
P l u n g e
happily into the unknown
and know
that no matter what wicked things
may come this way,
 with her life will be okay

RUN, MOON BOY, RUN

You can't bury the dead when they're living.
Sail from here, open the door and close it forever.

Run, you, through the snow and ice, watch it melt before
your eyes, as the memories and song you cherished
fade, out of shot, and witness, soon the frozen shell
around your heart will be nothing
but a puddle under a warm sun in paradise.

Depart this skull. Destroy your asinine persona.

CHAPTER 2. MOON BOY.

Under construction.

COLORBLIND CHAMELEON

Sometimes I feel
like a colorblind chameleon,
caught in a kaleidoscope
of constantly changing colors.

I'm unique but confused.

Can anyone tell me,
to which of these
billion hues
do I belong?

WEIRDO

I've been feeling distant,
out of place,
floating all day
next to people
in a river I don't belong.
I'm jealous,
how do they fit on this planet,
while I'm left
lost in space?

What's wrong with me?

I spend my nights
in a silent room,
alone in a bed
that keeps getting bigger.
I overthink, overanalyze—
consumed and haunted constantly
by voices that paint
pictures of heartache
across my brain.

What's wrong with me?

I'm lonely,
finding my place
in the wrong places.
Mishandling hearts, I'm sorry.
I'm just looking to be found.

I don't want to be alone,
but maybe I do—
more and more it becomes a norm.

What's wrong with me?

Tonight, I roll over
to a soft-skinned,
sweet smelling stranger.
She's cute, kind
and ready to go steady
—I'll lose touch not much later.

"WHAT'S WRONG WITH YOU, WEIRDO?"

FRESHMAN

Ninth grade was hard.
It felt like there were all these preset paths
I was trying to balance simultaneously,
then gosh-damn calamity struck
when all collided,
leaving a classic cartoon KABOOM!
with the big gray cloud
of smoke and debris,
and a broken
little boy
lost
 inside.

Pressures of academics and
ruthless
social codes consumed my heart and mind,
as I navigated a
world which had suddenly become
new to me, and whose complexity
seemed to
multiply overnight. It was
a
 barrage
of sensory chaos
leaving my feeble brain
running
five-thousand
miles per hour, overheated,
its wobbly, tired legs
somehow not collapsed and toppled,
despite the weight of gravity slowly
pulling me into a sad, suffocating black hole.

I found out how naïve I really was that year.
Life was a game of strategy and risk,
not love and community
like Big Bird
had led me
to believe. Though I didn't understand why
it was designated life need be so cruel,
I felt okay, then, knowing I and my twinkling irises
had yet been eyewitness to many moments
wherein glints of bright, changing
light and chroma were revealed
  — signals an irrefutable, obscure beauty
exists within the turmoil of life.

With this knowledge, I calculated only
one
logical conclusion:
  In a blink, I'll be here and gone,
  so why not?
I'll gear up, go ahead, play this
ancient VR game. I'll explore
as many crevices of this crazy world as I can.
Eventually, I'll find out what happens at
The End.

Soon, the summer of '05 was over.
I was a boxer in the ring ready to fight.
The bell rang for Round 2 of high school,
and that day,
I took my first steps
through the noise and the haze,
in search of the great mysterious unknown,
waiting for me
beyond my
  childhood horizons.

THE ESCAPE ARTIST

Observe and be astounded
Per the remarkably basic
Temporary
Mental hostage situation in my head

It's felt lately like my soul has
Been drowned in concrete
Unable to speak or breathe
Suffocating
Under walls of tsunami
Acid-rainwater falling
Falling
Falling,
 Submerging me like a sentimental Houdini

I'll be out free
In
No time

PRETTY

Care to help a boy in need, pretty please?
I've fallen for a girl, I'm pretty weak, and
I'm pretty sure this girl fell right out of my dreams.
She's the prettiest girl this world's ever seen—
prettier than the prettiest poetry ever spoken,
or the prettiest song listened.
She's my pretty piece of art, on her, I'm focused.
My hope is she's not too pretty to see me.
For, you see, I'm pretty sure if she could see
how pretty she is to me, maybe we could be together.
I could kiss her pretty face, and maybe,
in an ugly world, I'd make her pretty happy.

SPLATTERED PAINT

I'm a mess

Clothes, uncoordinated —
my colors mixed
like my personality

On the outside,
you see clean and calm, inside
lives chaos

Years ago, heavy bombs
EXPLODED,
and left me here hopeless, my paints
bleeding together creating
black where bright colors should be

Day after day, I do my best to tell myself
I am a masterpiece,
waiting hopefully for someone who
just might see
all the beauty inside
that I could never find

OH, BOTHER.

I'm depressed today
I'm depressed this whole month,
Apparently
And even more months after, maybe

I just checked,
Looks like I'll be depressed
Tomorrow, too

Where in the **black hole**
Fuck
Did my serotonin go?
Have I made another mental error–
Some tiny miscalculation
Somewhere slipped
Through the microscopic
Cracks of my maxed out mental defenses?

My lovely, glass noggin is,
At this moment,
A
Shiny,
Shattered puzzle

My deepest apologies, ladies and gentlemen,
As we experience our
Favorite
 Technical difficulties

SEROTONIN DEALER

Movie marathons, Finding a new favorite song
Cosmically radiant, magenta-purple flowers
just
casually
growing
on the side of the 15 Highway
Bubbles, and kids giggling
Mind-exploding, tropical sherbet swirls in the sky
for personal viewing pleasure
every morn' and nightly without fail
Night drives down barren roads
sneaking peeks into space and a black celestial sea
Happy dreams,
and
Fucking waking up on days off

MUDDY SHOES

In muddy shoes, it's so hard to move

Why am I stuck still standing in life's sludge,
while everybody else strolls along
on the concrete
nice and neat?

I really thought I knew where I was going
The path seemed so solid when I started
 — I swore I knew what I wanted

I think I'm lost now

I watch everyone around me happy, settled,
shuffling comfortably along,
but I still haven't found where I belong

I guess I'm just a weird
little kid walking in the mud

SUNBURNT MEMORIES

Vivid and radiant
—*yet grainy and blurred*—memories flash like
disposable camera film prints in my head
Sunburnt, orange and pink images washed
with crystal-aqua blue
and nostalgia take me to the beach
in 1996, swimming care-free
with cousins in shallow waves, which to us felt gigantic

I can feel my skin tinged by warm rays, ultra-violet,
and a cool, salty mist, as familiar, young voices
laugh and carry extravagant, adolescent conversations

The ocean breathes in, and exhales

I'm a six-ish year old again,
totally lost
in the pure beauty and bliss of being alive

JUMPING OUT OF PLANES

Wohhh —
okay, this is a little dangerous.
Whose idea even was this?

What is the sense in risking it all?

Why would she
deliberately
climb so far and high
just to fall and risk — what if
she missed? With no parachute
to save her, she would crash
ten thousand miles an hour
down into the ground,
her broken heart obliterated
by the person
who swore to catch her

For you, though—
you special m.f.—
for you,
risks be damned,
she jumps
from the moon and stars into love
with you withholding nothing,
offering the entirety
of herself
to you . . .

What do you do now? That's
right, big dummy,

jump too

Throw away your parachute.
Tell every cynical voice
in your head
to *STFU!*

and jump

And then you go—
unsparingly,
you HOLD her
PROTECT her
You LOVE her
with every last atom in your body,
until time and space
washes
 your body
away

CHAPTER 3. COLOR.

The colors of my world.

GRAYISH GRAY

Bland little boy,
you're such a faded gray mess
What happened to the days long ago
when you still had your neon glow and
your bright and blinding smile
shined freely?

It was truly beautiful, infectious,
your prismatic grin. Your aura was
like a gorgeous kaleidoscope blazing
across the cosmos
spitting vivid sparks, pure joy

Tell me, dull one, when was it that you lost
your colorful bubble? What terrible thing
turned you to this grayish gray bum who
can't smile—even though he has no reason
not to? Who put you in this monochrome room playing
grayish blue tunes trying to feel
something inside? Who made your heart dead
and desert-dry like your eyes? *Why won't your
tears do what they're supposed to?*

I'm sorry, I'm not comprehending, what awful hurt
could have possibly incurred
to leave this twisted spell spreading
charcoal over every inch of your once
psychedelic
soul?

What worthless, vile ghosts stole every trace of
color from your spirit's beautiful flame? Explain,
what GIANT WAVE crashed down
upon your **burning** brilliance to make it all fade
away—leaving nothing
in its wake but murky, muddy seafoam?

My sad, bland boy . . .
 is it too late to pull you back into the light?
When you look in the mirror, can you
spot a flicker of color still inside your eyes?
Like the sunrise
after a cold, *cloudy* night,
will you return soon to me,
resurrected in radiant blues, pinks, and purples
in the wet morning sky?

SPACE-LOOT

Everything I write is simply paraphrase to
Life's multidimensional language of prisms,
and this documentary on reality
which came pre-installed in my
RNA, buried deep like a hidden treasure.

I'm over the gold rush.
I wish to butterfly and backstroke in living colors
until I die

PENTHOUSE POOL DISCO

There's an inside pool on
the top of my head.
I dive in everyday and swim. Inside
this pool are colorful chemicals, which
mix and react with each encounter and hour
passing. Though the colors
are not always pretty,
and the water sometimes cold, I jump
and swim, still, from sunrise
to nightfall, because the pool reminds me
that
 I am alive.

By some cosmic stroke of luck,
I am here drenched in
life and refractive, non-synthetic feelings.

BLUE FRUIT

Be blue, you strange fruit
Be gray, or royal purple, like thunderous,
midsummer night
skies,
 should you need to

Be of hues vibrant, or that of matte - if you want
Be wavy as the green tops of palm trees
Be winter morning blue
Be not worried what lost souls
perceive
of the colors you learn
Cherish the miracle of your oft-buried
psychedelic soul
 — and protect it

On the days the black goo begins to creep across
your slimy pink,
remind thine self —
much like the white sun from time to time —
you, too, are allowed a hush
eclipse
via solitude and shuttered curtains,
while the Earth basks
 in the abstract brilliance of *hue*

SUN BATH

Here comes the eternally burning
ball of hydrogen
gas
to swallow up, envelope
in roaring licks of fire,
 this astronomic fleck
of existence

I wonder, in these last moments,
my soul and its impending fate . . .
Perhaps its gravity and the sun's
shall collide,
collapse and implode,
folding
infinitely, christening
the greatest black-hole birthday!

Or, maybe it is to simply evaporate
inside a gurgling bath of neon yellow x-rays
and
plasma

ORANGE JELL-O

Eurythmic audio bounces my body mass
like orange Jell-O in my room,
while I slide atop tiny lightning
across the room's frizzy brown carpet in my socks.
I'm swimming in hyper-hydrated, electronic vibrations
currently dancing up, down, and around my every limb—
jiggling my head, like a funky
sunflower
 to the summer wind's falsetto.

Universe, you are one *groovy* mf.

It is long past the hour of slumber,
but here vibes, I, listening to hand-picked playlists
and the soft carve of tires gliding over asphalt outside.

PLUM SPRINKLES

Time for wine to splash over
bruises of black cherry tint smudged across
and
over this heart,
my resilient property

Tonight, the echoes of melancholy
drown in the mighty current of my blissfulness

This odd man is happier
than a bank account with no kids on Christmas,
here, beside the embodiment of divine perfection
vibing, together with me, in neon blue-and-yellow socks
— she, sent to me supernaturally . . .
Two dazzling, chocolate-glazed-donut colored
irises, heart and soul harmonized exquisitely
to my energy mixtape and circadian rhythm

Though this foolish world go up and down
in plum-tinged, littery embers –
until all life endeth,
 nothing else remaineth but
 peace and royal blue skies, with you

LUNCH DREAM

I'm on my lunch break,
just killed a big plate of bomb food

"What to do now?" I'm thinking.
I'm bored, kind of wishing
I could turn this cafeteria into a playground.

Picture this:
stimulus deprived, I'd
splash zesty lemon yellows on the wall
Electric-blue twisty slides might descend
like waterfalls from the top floor
all the way to the bottom

Screw it,
put a ball pit to drop in
Make sure those plastic balls are bright and vivid
I'm picturing rainbows exploding
like Dippin' Dot ice cream when I dive in

Pump gallons and gallons of paint
onto the floor,
so we can slip, slide, and glide across,
while simultaneously turning our
sharp business suits
and nice ties
to beautiful tie-dye works of art

I want ten fully loaded dump trucks
to pull up and flood the room
with a million balloons
Neon pool noodles and giant beach balls
would replace tables and chairs
Picture disco balls and strobe lights
hanging from the ceiling
spitting lasers everywhere!

With wild eyes,
I'd scream out, *"FOOOOD FIGHT!"*

then swiftly launch my cheesecake flavored

Greek yogurt across the room
to hit the face

of whom it may concern

What a shame and a bummer
it's all in my head, though . . .

If these visions really came to fruition,
a declaration of great urgency would be issued
"NO CLOCKS ALLOWED" it would say -
like this little tick-tick-tick-tick-ticker
who so rudely just announced
the fate of my lunch time

Yes, sadly, I'm all out of minutes,
says the digits
on my watch's tiny face

So, my lame, plain lunch bag
gets packed and zipped up

Pop goes the bubble on my crazy dream,
as I walk my butt back
to my boring old seat
to do boring work things-
WAAACK!

POCKET MONSTERS

Highlighter
yellow-green Gameboy loading screens,
care-free, clueless to the mystery, what waited.
Time, at the mercy of a pocket-sized gaming system . . .

Ignorance was bliss. Apologies. I'm learning as I go.

I'd had a dream to barrel through the tall grass, course
uninterrupted. But the battles cannot be skipped,
and again,
 here I spin in mental limbo.

Will you stay with me on this loading screen?

LEAKY GOGGLES

What is life without light - but a grave?

Fix your goggles, good man, the lighthouses are
frozen.
The lifeboats are gone.

Society has castrated your eye-balls with an
ice-cream scoop, serving up ozone-depleting,
chocolate-dipped shit to legions of milky-eyed
children
masquerading in their finest, invisible
grown-up garments,
 frolicking in charred darkness believing it day

In the end, this world's greedy beloved will
sob
and cry furiously unto THEE, in grand irony:

You devoured the nutty rocky-road with glee.
You killed us. . . .

as the copper-red curtain of dusk
begins to set to glacial black, and quasi-tragically,
our titanic planet merrily, merrily sloshes down
humanity

Soak in every sun-ray and RGB you can find, kids.

ZOMBIELAND

Sadly, red is a color that loves to drip
The red once coursing, warmly, inside
intricate veins
to my abnormal heart is gone

Red reflections
of a zombie whose intentions were good

Oh, selfish thing, with your long-spoiled empathy . . .
LOOK at the damage—*your doing!*

Run now, please,
to the void you belong, Monster,
and forever thereafter, as briny streams polluted
by silt makeup the color of dried blood
drip
from her bloodshot eyes and cheeks –
until they drip no more, and
you are but a ghost in a youthful scary story

I want to live in the TV

It seems chill in there
No goodnight
No goodbyes
Body made of *flickering* lines of static
Strolling around
Inside the black box of unlimited
Living the lives of people whom hath never lived
Anchored forever in the LED sea, dark and bright like my soul

GROOVY BABY

You're so groovy, baby
 Come a little closer to me, baby

I want to know how'd you get so cool,
and can I have me some of these
neon-phantasmical
vibes you're radiating,
looking all cute and sunshine-like?

Your soul must be where rainbows come from*!*
Your love is a drug, spinning my neurons
into
colorful, cosmic fiestas*!*

I want to jump inside your dazzling energy wave,
and swim within your perfectly irregular galaxy
until infinity
swallows this beautiful world **whole**

How groovy life is with you, baby
 — one day you'll be my wife, groovy baby

YOU ARE THE COLOR OF LIFE TO MY CORNEA

You are the aqua-blue moon which shined on seductive eyes in May. You are hypnotic strobe lights showing the dance floor in darkness.

You are the neon-cyan fruit tree I found beaming in the city; incandescent roots nourish my hungering heart and skeleton.

You are cool water caressing me afloat in the Pacific; in your midst, speed limits are scarcely seen.

You are the perfect color for any outfit in our closet.
You are — *according to science and statistics,* impossible.
You are thirst-quenching.
You are the **billowy**, lemon-blue tent by the cove
where time drank refreshing mellow beats and
Mexican beers for a *siesta* . . .

You are the phantasmical painting I've got my head dunked inside, whose vibrating, blue-tinted blonde highlights that spring evening
 changed this man's very direction on the planes
of existence.

PSYCHEDELIC COMET

Alien in a dress, where you going?
Four-wheels-a-foot,
opalescent earrings,
slicing through sheets of gentle breeze
like
enchanted scissors,
 sidewalk sailing in your classic
cosmic-black skates

What interstellar sorcery compels
solar light beams to materialize,
shimmy and cha-cha
so playfully and precisely
behind this sweet, caramel-drizzled
figurine, who so charmingly carves summer oxygen –
orbiting,
 so closely, the space-coordinates of my heart?

Have I told you I love you?

Your smile is psychoactive; I think I'm rolling too . . .
Visions of a psychedelic comet with her tail of endorphins,
and love-laced, chemical bubbles
bathing the pipes of my
primitive
body and brain

How did a wee crum in the fabric
of
reality
 end up getting so lucky?

I want to swim, for the rest of my weekends,
in your cotton-candy nebula
—

I don't know astrology, but thank the stars,
Mars, Venus, and every moon
you found me;
seconds here feel infinite

TWENTY-EIGHT MINUTES LEFT ON THE ROAD, WEDNESDAY

The sky is a muddy film
Colors are deaf, the blues—heavy brown,
pulling me deep into chasms of marbled, beige emotion

Gravity is dirty-gold, luster, weathered
by burdens of time
crashing against my windshield. God smeared
stale coffee across my blanched cerebral cortex

LOOK, the racer's genetically-modified
third-eye droops, slow, out-of-focus —
Yesterday and the present
are out of reach,
 so it strains for tomorrow

POLAR SNOW-ANGEL

Notebook paper plane,
 send notice: *To angel in human disguise –*

You have stirred the sleeping aurora lights
of
red marrow's summit,
just north of shouldered peaks

Ever since these two perpendicular timelines
of ours bumped axis, looming skull-clouds
all
parallel
part, like tamed hurricanes,
in the presence of my beloved
Her kisses, lush like vanilla cream froth on
hot-*chocolaté*
 Lips of powdered mochi and soft-falling snow
at dusk

Together, we create a four-dimensional
pocket of peace in the space around us
—

Beside thee, my ego is spaced out,
high—*as our hotboxed-climate,*
on this fragrance of love we're lying in

I wished on an ultraviolet star in another galaxy
that so it should be:
For as long as the universe shall allow it,

we will crash through the slopes of time like
badass
avalanches
Be it in elegant attire, my darling,
 or sweatpants, and sweater adorned

THE FOREST OF TOMORROW ENVELOPES THE ATOMS OF OUR SOULS

I bask in trails of cinnamon embers and oxygen at your

Skirt side

You lovely green fireball from the cosmos

Jungle princess

Accompanied a wary foreigner into Él Dorado

Swam me under secret falls, sweet as *sandía*

Kissed my heart with tanged hips and lips

Singing, soothingly, songs adrip in your curious

Vibrations

I love you

My warrior of sol and waters

Mountain of Central American evergreens

You planted a sunrise inside me . . .

I've found I desire to climb more of tomorrow's branches

 And

Swing over this lush current with you

Hold your breath

Until the rainforest loses its very last species of lumber,

Would you marry me?

CHAPTER 4. LOVE LETTERS FROM SPACE.

Dedicated to my sea and sun, Marisol.

The sea and the sun.

How appropriate it is to me that your name
should be
as beautiful and magnificent as your soul,
and how lovely the calm you bring to me,
like the tropical scene of sea and sun that your name's
seven letters equal

A perpetual daydream, still —
how you found me, and I you —
as if these two infinitely random paths of ours
were actually drawn before began the universe itself

Through the frost and flurry, darkness and despair,
for so long, I pulled and pulled and pulled on this
volatile cosmic string,
wading waist-deep into the colorful, cloudy unknown,
my ravaged mind at war for peace, blindly and
faithfully believing every moment is a moment
meant to be, reminding myself again and again
that even were I *not* to take the road I'd hoped,
everything happens for a reason
— happiness would be my destination

And then, like inside some heavy dream,
just beyond the deepest depths of my imagination,
amidst infinite burning stars and glittering space-dust,
a gift from God, I found you,
'my sea and sun'
Mi Marisol

PROTOSTAR

I see you. *Stellar-woman, thou should not exist*

I believe I have slipped into a dream
Shh. *Either I, you, or us should not be here*

Me wonders if we unlocked some primeval
combination, cracked a 5th-wall and
>>> phased into long-term, non-fiction fantasy

Since your presence, the monsters in the mirror
wear grins and coat shimmering, in garden, full
bloomed.
Each smells like floral conditioner.
Don't worry, I'll not speak, should you neither.

Can we be irrational?

Mythic-entity of many a day and night dream,
will you come hither and marry these lips
of spirited electrons? What if we couple of
soular astronauts, in 1 - 3 business days,
blasted off in dusted white
rocket to combine two rogue worlds in orbit?

Imagine if you do: I, you, us — moonroof, slid in,
snapping infinite galaxy pics, albums aflood with
chroma shots: two strange planets
fizzed
in milky radio waves, and atomic love . . .

Can you feel it?
Lady Luck, she again beckons, my royal crush.
Shall we play the next hand?

Let stained glass shine on gold-doubled onyx rings,
says your energy surfer. Track a few miles
aside me and reflective blacktop, next weekend . . .

Outheld hand. You slipped in for the immortal night.

Afore white linen-sheets, neon-lights call, **buzzing** –
my nebula empress,
 the desert moon awaits

GROWN UP

So, this is it, huh, baby—
this warm, cozy feeling you give me?
It seems reminiscent
of freshly-brewed coffee
in the morning
with my favorite creamer

You know,
when the sweet from the sugar
is just the right degree,
you're there blissfully inhaling
the most heavenly of steam,
then you gently *sip*, and
BING!
the heat washes over your heart
as it crosses your lips
  — you get me?

I mean, *basically*,
what I'm saying is:
a waterfall—NO,
a "JAVA-fall"
of your favorite
(specially-picked)
upscale store-bought,
piping hot,
caramel-roasted goodness
cascading
down my esophagus
splashing
right into my gut
 is what you feel like

Divine aroma — my comfort in a cup
Every morning for the rest of my life,
I want your scent
infused into my bed
when I wake up

So natural,
sustainable,
you are to me
Feels like cheap pills
on weary taste buds
I'd been placing

Sparkly artificial highs only
tantalize the naïve mind
Never had a clue how terribly
my soul was
starving

I was waiting for rain in a dry Sahara,
so dehydrated,
for so long,
on my synthetic image of love

This you and me thing, though,
feels grown up
I'm so insanely glad you showed up

I PROCLAIM
my gratefulness to the heavens!
 I thank God, for the gift He's given!

 This is love—and I love you,
baby boo

EUROPA ON THE SOFA

I have been to the moons of Jupiter;
I love you all the way there, and back, again, again.

The number of orbits passed waiting
for you, I really don't recall. I only know
that, now, I long to stop time
and spend a kajillion
light-years riding
through life's cosmic waves with you.

Europa on the sofa,
while you *Arche* your back;
under
meteor-hot showers, two lovers,
you and me,
lost in our own dimensions.

My moon was lonely before,
but now you're right here during
its dark times. If I haven't said it already,
I am totally in love with you, moon glow.
I need you to know,
though I previously thought it
not comprehensively possible,
you make this peculiar lunar kid
finally feel **WHOLE**—
like the fully-charged,
big, white night-light in the sky
which visits every month. I appreciate
your fine
reflection.

HOOKED

We're a bit strange, are we not – we couple of
orange-purple tulips river-dancing in adjoined creeks?

As if there were no waterfall waiting for us beneath
the metallic, copper horizon—we fucking bloomed,
in most
raging
 rapids of time

How many hours, I fumbled in bleak tundra –
until whence I found upon thine heart's hot-springs?

You've the ability to make a *fern* flower
Mi agua de **sunshine**

Hotter than boiling hibiscus, you light the snarled and
overgrown walls
of my most protected insides
with luminescent blue-green fire

You have me over the moon's flowers, my alien female

I've been hooked. I'm home.

Pinky promise kiss, in tropical luster and serenity,
in jungles' loudest rain —
nay, all-between —
I will hold firm and protect your luscious roots

HER SOUNDTRACK

Her.
It all starts with Her.
This room I'm sitting in is too loud.
Too many people, too many voices,
but her . . .
 she steps in and the music starts.

Does She know? *Can She hear it?*

The music engulfs the room in a symphonic flood,
and I think they can hear it too. The people, the voices,
they're SILENT,
but it's an orchestra—
an explosion of sound that I'm hearing.

The piano builds up gradually, playing along
to her every step, as she walks so softly, slowly,
closer and closer to me —
MY HEART IS POUNDING!
It's beating so fast, it's a full-on sprint!

And, now, the piano's lost control!
I swear I hear black and white ivory keys
somewhere out of sight going crazy to the beat!

Her.

Amidst the harmonic madness, the room is still.

Everyone is silent, watching Her.
The beautiful sound I hear
has surrounded Her and everything around Her.
Surely, GOD has composed this—
this song that caresses Her face so gently
yet simultaneously FILLS the room with a **CRASH** of percussion.

She's reached my seat now. I'm breathless.

The piano s l o w s down . . .

AND SPEEDS UP!
And I'm stuck.

Lost in this ocean of beauty and sound before me.

Her . . .

She leans down towards me. Those notes as
She did will play in my head for infinity, and beyond that.

a peck

She kissed me . . .
and the orchestra of piano, percussion, and instruments
ERUPTS uncontrollably!

And the people are gone. The world is gone.
Like a lucid dream, it's just me
and Her—
and it's perfect.
She's perfect.
It's all so. damn. perfect.

. . .

"Why are you always so extra, babe!"
bashfully demands my girlfriend
— the grinning angel now standing before me.

"Shhh . . ." I smile, and whisper in a silly trance.
"Just let the music play, baby. Just let the music play . . ."

LOVE DRUNK

You make me feel
like a kid who just got a brand-new bike
I kind of forgot what this felt like
For you, I think I'd drive a thousand miles
California, Arizona, Ohio, or I don't know —
you're here, so how about we just save the gas?
Lately, you make me want to be romantic,
bouquets and candles on the top of my list
Love songs all day, all they do is talk about you
Your face in my brain stays on a loop
You're beautiful beyond my wildest dreams
I think about you at night while I'm lying in bed
You're my reason to wake and my reason to sleep
You're my daydream, my nightdream,
my lunch dream, my nap dream
 — *you're my dream come true*
All roads led to you, and I'm so thankful
A big butterfly family in my gut goes crazy
when I see you
How did I get so lucky?
You're so imperfect, it's perfect
You fit in my life like that one weird piece
that finishes the puzzle
I love you,
I trust you,
and I'm not scared to
You're my sun girl, you're out of this world
You're intoxicating, addicting
If you catch me staring, forgive me,
I'm just so lost, I forgot
what this felt like . . .

DIVINE CHEMISTRY

Euphoria. I think God had a plan and you
were born with four souls more than
everyone, because He knew
that I would need
 each
 and
 every
 one
to hold this supernova-size joy and light
I was missing but which you now leave
spinning
furiously,
like moon and sun,
day and nightly, inside my heart.

Adrift in a dark universe, I'd been,
previous to our serendipitous union.
Now, though,
like electrons and protons,
I vow to spend the rest of my life reciprocating
all seven octillion highly-attractive atoms of yours
with nothing but love and energy. **You are my euphoria.**

HIGH TIDE

Tonight,
rivers
flow into rivers
flowing into waterfalls falling into rivers
flowing into
oceans
 of endless, unfiltered love for you

You are the moon, and I, the captive tide,
rising to the pull of your crescent lips,
drunk on their luscious gravity
and
summer night spirits

LATE NIGHTS, LAUGHING WITH YOU

I am extremely hard on myself
So much so, I believe in my heart if I somehow
printed the transcripts of my inner monologues
to be read out audibly, were your poor ears to hear,
you would shed rivers, for certain—
your heart
more and more broken
with each ozone-cold word, syllable, repeated
aloud

Try as I might, I've learned
I just won't always be able to put
the volume
to
 zero
on this chaotic, low-budget
ESPN commentary in my head
But, whenever you
y yo estamos juntos,
you are my universal remote
with this magic MUTE button
I can count on always
for the most intensely
bright
and silent moments of peace
my beat-up brain
wasn't sure existed
before you danced into my life

Sweet Baby Jesus, I just want to say,
thank you, Lord,
for this incredible woman next to me,
for the joy her smile radiates,

and for her heart-melting laugh, which I crave
—like vanilla ice cream sandwiches for breakfast,
lunch,
 and dinner

Laundromat on Cesar Chavez

I got our baskets

Loud machines, music, voices clamorous, garbled
Swirling are soap water and anonymous lives of thread
Resting stop for timelines, trapped in a pause, surreal

Brilliant work, creator

All's dark and lovely as it must be

The chaos of noise is drowned, scrubbed in suds
Me, kissed, selected by Her trusting, giving heart
Neck
Waist
Fingers

To our playlist, in a dream of a day, fold each, fold
Always, I am your partner to wash, fold each, fold
Garments, blankets, or towels, fold each fold
Dirty hours to pure
No palm empty
Magic and wishes rinsed in reality, fold
You, sunniest, completion
At last, the full load of white clothes

QUEEN TACO

There's been a delay in my neural link.

I let imperfect words free upon thee;
sent them sprattling in disarray to your poor,
beautiful, almond-butter complexion, once again.

Terrific.

Let begin yet another descent into my over-cultivated
concern for a narrative unworthy...

BUT HARK, ye olde Anxiety,
my words are translated. Nay,
my recipient, fluent — speaking back,
in fresh mango tongue,
gentle words, always, when they're needed.

You make me believe I'm not defective.

YOU, señorita, are the sunlight
at the end of every
tunnel
on this
roller-coaster twirling through the cosmos,
where to each other, the universe sat we lovebirds next.

I love you, I love you as crazy as this burning world,
and more. I am The King, and you are The Queen –
equally of
all the land's tacos,
our home,
 and my heart.

PLAYER 2

We're a little more different than we thought.
Exciting revelations about our two characters. Rewards.
More I never knew a clue about love.

Befer vanilla wax had dripped; learnt I was flammable.

My altered ego blows smoke, but embers farther spread.
Infer no more, honesty-fueled, you turn the critic to fan.
I love you, and on through brittle flesh I burn to feel this.
To touch your string.
Your body of fire blushing.
 Spilled sun colors oozing into our weeks, being.
We scouts of truth's secrets.

You're A Salad.

Refrigerator cool, baby

Washed green, iceberg fresh

Exquisitely chippy cucumber

Almond skin

Sliced, honey apple cheeks

Cheese levels great

Baking bit by bit my frozen fibers

Sweet and spicy dressing on my mustache

LA LOTERÍA

The experience's bizarre, audible. Buttercream ranch on
fast food tacos. This is explosive in every cell, piercing
through magnified nanoseconds. I'm slow, but it's rapid,
lifting.
Feels like all of all things flowing up in two strait bodies.
Above the veil and across shrinking mountains, going.
A ride not possibly dreamed or imagined, our love,
a calvary through
time, the freak of nature bowing.

I belong to you. Take my smoothed pieces apart,
you hold my heart in balance.

See, and soul.

I am so faulty, draining, pended amplifying repairs.
Your gripped embrace, currently, is jumpstarting
a broken battery.
We lost, but just one card. We're winning wildly, baby.
Tengo la sol y mar, mi lotería.

A Sunday afternoon with Marisol

Silver chill, in the bed, each other, side-to-side, morning hair dripping, perfect degree to have your hand in hand. Golden-orange curtains hide the day's mystery rays. The hour is a ten, eleven, two moving through dream life. We do, we don't, the dishes. Movie, nonlinear magic, stars.

Lounge, or bucket seats through our merging worlds.

25 cents, unlock 250 scents, waves of fresh in our room and dreams. Who'd allow such Lovely ifn't Love, Literal? Holy lens, I cherish this. I know not 5, even 605, hours of coming traffic could crash into here, our exotic pocket of perfect cruising in the carpool of spacetime. I love

you.

Beach sun.

What's your favorite activity when not being perfect?

Honey buns.
We exist now, so we exist forever.
On the prowl of plots together making stories collected.

We dance a little different,
never the metronome choreographed
one another's
erratic soles.

If you can loop in space, you can loop in time;
were you waiting for me?

Fingers, red hot, wrapped around my heart, it died, but
you sparked a secret circuit. Outlet engulfed. Spicy
feline. You run the sun. Tamed the flying lion.

Wide-arch'ed bridge to love.
Light the loopholes, and show me the way.

HEY SLEEPING BEAUTY

While we taco majesties slumber,
I want these words printed in constellation
to guide you should the sun be ever swallowed black:

I fucking love you

You are a dream radiating reality,
walked up by the universe to light my two right-feet.

Thank you

Thou assembled the puzzle, completed my life's riddle,
catalyst of my nude soul rediscovered.

Doze soundly under ambient Eastern lights.
A kiss comes, sailing to you across heaven's lake.
When your eyelashes flutter in this night's mid,
may
you
fall
only deeper in dream of creamy soft-serve in the
stratosphere,
 oh broad-eyed, luminary butterfly.

MARISÓL

My lush little chica de la sol
How I adore the cute way she says CHICAGO

In a steamy home, clarity brews to life's blurry lens
There is warmth in your sparkling aqueous

Tomorrow and today dance unphased on high-wires
While we chug along into the next level

Yearly folded, weekly, daily
I gaze upon thine lips' puckered corners
Thine ego-melting, kaleidoscope eyes
Unable to contain a grin at our waterside dives
Cloudtop bike rides and
Every curve we've slung this clock around together

I pray time is a baby sea turtle with nowhere to be
So, slow, they flitter to hover and watch us for awhile

CHAPTER 5. VOLUME.

Loud, **quiet.**

THIS IS FINE.

*I say, what good fortune that
our every thought
be not scribed to paper, isn't it?*

*There's enough smoke and flames in California,
spared
a Jurassic-forest bonfire
smoldering round and round the broken
cuckoo clock*

CLAUSTROPHOBIC ASTRONAUT

Will your vapid ocean of worries be in vain?

So many questions you'll never have the time to answer.

Insistently asking, always asking, asking.

Mission control screams, all is clear, but you don't hear,

opaque helmet sealed, stippled by hourglass sand, astro

white

and black,

blasted

inside a lonely singularity . . .

You see the vibrant infinity of stars burning — and even

more

dark matter.

Poor, beaten, space cowboy.

Your reflective mask, you've worn, relatively, how long?

Airtight, layered, unload this unrequired weight off.

Young male of moons, running nowhere in suffocated

space boots, mouth prone frozen by lack of oxygen, and

wild imagination.

Thy subconscious, fixated on bluing gray noise.

Why doth the ghost in your ear deny you peace?

With your toasted eyes, peek: a position of safety.

CAN YOU HEAR ME?

Life or death, you clutch to the ground for control.

Gentle-being, lived so long in your black hole.

Release your shiny headpiece, your protective suit now.

See

salt

crystals blob, and breathe. Fill your wide ribcage

with alien weightlessness. Let your brain drink,

quenched;

cheers to the future.

Astronauts don't belong on Earth, rise and glide

untethered.

HEY, IT'S ME AGAIN.

Hey,
I'm sorry
for sounding so generic,
and repetitive…
but,
it's me again. Two inches less than
5'10", black hair, brown eyes,
striding around my planet real
chill-like, meanwhile
my cranial jukebox
up top jankily
bounces and bangs. Day,
night,
and morn,
to my perturbed dismay,
 the noise comes and it goes,
every voice, my own,
 volume up, volume down,
A BROKEN RECORD
 spinning and playing as we speak,
just me
questioning me about
every fucking
thing
of everything,
forever
and ever
 —and ever, it'd seem . . .

Chin up, though.

Such a *pretty* soul, Mr. Mirror—
 for what reason, do you think,
 does this brain so oft
 treat us
 so
 ugly?

BREIGH-BORLY PEOPLE

I'm so sleepy. Can you pretend I'm invisible?

Sorry, the muscles for feigned grinning hibernate;
this is not a safe-space for your quarrels toward reality

Go find a wasted other miniature ass-hole
with lackluster
thoughts
better suited for your juvenile stool and vomit

I'm sleepy.
I wish, to an extraordinary degree,
life
ought not
 have made us meet

You're severely annoying;
I've no imagination to spare for the temper
tantrums
of eroded limbic systems

So oblivious to your ugliness.
Yes, I realize there's no other more important than
you, beyond the inflated particle in space-
time of which
ye currently inhabit . . .

Lethargy in these brown eyes –
I am sleepy. I'm leaving.

Swallow your dense carbon dioxide elsewhere,
and perish in
history absent statue, fossil, and imprint,
save the rigid stick climbing your soft, cushy
anus

WORKING ON SATURDAY

The sun has made its bittersweet arrival and
these blankets have ingested the weight of the moon,
as they hug me now with the tenderness of
cotton balls and silk clouds coaxing my eyelids
to slip and fall back asleep. Back to the world of
strange adventures and vivid dreams
I left—not of my own accord—which waits for me,
a mere breath away, should I tilt
ever so slightly to the side and pull this comforter
infused in the warmth of two sleepy lovers
over
my shoulder
 to embrace the slumber
I so desire. . .

NARRATORS:

Narrator, we all are,
to each transition in our stream of time;
I have
Narrators, each my own

Narrators, you've got one too
You listen
and
discourse, also, over every shoulder shift,
hip fidget, and finger twitch –
I assume,
 lest I be odd

My
Narrators say—

**Narrators can't narrate with playing music, it
drowns them out usually. I've no desire to delete
mine, I'm
aware my
Narrators love me, but some days, and considerable
minutes, I just wish I had a way to mute the bouquet
of Narrators living in cold craters between both earlobes*

Exercise

Everyday.
Every muscle.
Eat rations plated perfectly, eye nutritional facts.
Evolutionary wonder, dig your hole and chortle to the
elegant audience's direction turning soil under thin glass
elevated sunshade, punching heart through your chest.
Earned coins make all worthy of bruise, too, warped iris.
Etched, shaken, removed. Blast off the block, big stride,
Earth sliced a new early glimmer, another, another day
eroding for sake of continuity, but woe, you are so shot,
even the nicer face are diluting blur. Whipping o'er old
elephant's hurdles for weekends, chomp chomp chomp,
eat your bacon bits and corn, zoom. You and whisperers
end up a whippersnapper at neckbreak speed, whiplash.
Exploding calves, fall with eloquence, hip first, in, out,
echoes of the bedtime, say goodnight, good morning sir.
Ever never frown the sound; bounced off softest foot-
extruded blankets before the outside flare has even
exited its sweated covers, step. Curse the forced pressure
eloquent tongue and babble on dribble for a paragraph
eternal while you scavenge on the scrounge for sentences
expired. Play, cry, flip, emanate, drive, hike, stroll, scroll,
East, West, rise, lift, push, turn, sit, rest, read, tear,
envelope every cup of existence in big volume, or fade.
Emails, expectations, scraping in constant checkmate.
Eight day for the price of two, shrug the inside voices, O
exterminator of weakness, and pirouette bravehearted
each discounted week for the keys and credits. Thread
enamel, one by one through twenty, on, music quieting
ears ringing with flocks of pissy boy's parrots, dream.
Either live it or don't, player.

LOVER BOY IN SPACE

Deep in space,
the lover boy drifts lonely,
just floating,
watching
his freshly cracked
helmet screen

As red warning lights flicker,
oxygen trickles,
trickles,
and trickles
His ship slowly
 drifts farther and farther away

No sound—such a shame
Not even music to play,
as time, so unsympathetic,
casually
continues
ticking ticking
down.

Down.
Down.
Down.

Down . . .

Poor, lonely lover boy
in space,
how lovely a visitor would be today

MAKE IT STOP!

He's turning the volume on their mics up HIGHER.

Despite this convoluted room in my brain already
reverberating from the noisy three, or ten, internal
voices *yapping* away, commentating on
every. single. insignificant subject or sound detectable
in my vicinity, as some fifty or so
invisible shop lights on steroids are
pulsing PULSING pulsing
around me, so inconsiderate, humming ominously
louder
and louder
AND LOUDER. All the while I'm trying to decipher the
thousands of conversations being had by a thousand
microscopic buzzing flies inside my head, which
in reality, are all just me criticizing
MY EVERY THOUGHT AND DECISION
— no matter how mundane or minute.

He's turning the volume up and locking me inside,
and he is me,
and I don't know why.

EMOTE

Glitching alongside dusk lit storefronts
Silent, bloodcurdling hiss seethes from both ear canals
Sand bags on my head no longer feel light
Eroded sunwashed street signs, neither, make sense
Survive, solely says the GPS in the midst of a theme park
Freak of nature
Sinking into set cement
Exists in an invisible black pixel of the universe,
Yet convinced, by cruel beasts, the weight of life is his

Hours and emotes taste synthetic
Tomorrow and death come and go
We're all just crushed space dust

THIS IS NOT FINE.

Fury slams forward bursted upwards in fire-detonated demolish of hope or future, I rupture. Dismantled in lava waves. Ash and flash rain.

Billowing.

SYSTEM CRASH

> I can't talk right now

> There's a white, silent static and crackle

> Where all my words used to be. Please

> Forgive these technical difficulties

> I'm turning it off and on again

> And we'll see what happens <zzz>

6:37PM

My bed's not made, as it often isn't.

As you read this,
silky gray sheets lay scrumpled, exposed
by fleece blankets
jumbled up
 and tossed to the side—even though
I had plenty of time this morning
to leave them fixed and arranged, looking nothing
less than elegant and neat. There's
a wrinkled black shirt on the oatmeal-colored
brown carpet floor,
laying
on top of white ankle socks
that I forgot to put away, right next
to my favorite WFH black Nike slides,
used daily,
because in the early AM, I'm frequently lazy.
The heat currently sulking about the room
is no joke, but two feet from my face,
my stand-up fan spins it well, while
blinds lined perpendicular
to my wide-open window sway and clack,
putting the fading sunlight and dusty blue skyline
on full display for me.

6:37 in the evening, now,
 on my messy bed's edge I sit,
 just waiting for the hour and minutes
 on my watch to
flip.

TOP-LOAD HEAVY

Turn this frigid spin-cycle off. I WANT TO GET OUT.
How many loads of clean clothes,
before I'm granted freedom from the shrill and crash?

I'm tired of being a narcissistic mess of dirt and cold
water . . . I think it's better we don't talk about it.
WHY, WHY DOES THIS DRAINED WHIRLPOOL
ENSUE? It's cramped, cold,
and closed in,
 and a cycle-neverending.

Smash my faulty washer with an axe and hammer,
por favor,
over and over and over and over, until the mangled
old walls collapse and fly everywhere,
and a happy kid spills out.

Crash a new car through this viscous machine.
Come on, blow it up like a science project.
Get me out
Get me out
Get me out
My head's sopping wet.

Fucking punt me off the highest crater, so I can sleep
where sodden thoughts blossom.
You needn't to worry, just do it — it's under warranty.

Hurry, before the next cycle starts and the bleach swims.
Let me out
Let me out
Let me out
Let me out
Let me out
Let me out
Break the door and my femurs, take my shoes and these
loose drum screws, make the banging silent and my
brain deaf. AM I CLEAN, YET?

How long can I talk about myself?

Yipping is unpleasant for even two seconds over four.
I hear mine always. No event be too trivial for a yip or
seventy-three if I've fed a mid night's sleep. I promise,
I don't consciously aim to rhyme, but it sounds better.
Yippee, I'm narcissistic, the science sound on all sides
of the raucous. Negative feedback is old news. Locked,
rooftop, in an explosive safe. Yip for missed gaze, yip
for huffed chuckle misplaced, yip for poor words, yip
at yipping for missing responses. Turn the yip off. Who
are we? Yuck. Now, why so meek? Nothing's permanent.
These thoughts aren't a choice, oh well, they're laced
with consequences. *I hear I should take the onslaught of
slit under my face; the blender can't be touched.* I can't
see myself without the mirror. Close analysis never quite
looks at things clearly—yipping, the same for hearing.
Too much focus. Nothing feels real, sunk in this domed
circle of multiple yippers who know too much, yes.
Charge or power off blinking 5 percent, unpredictably.
Could you ignore the radio waves, when they roar inside
your head? I still don't get me yet. Let's take this exit.
Yip yip.

QUARTZ

Still water on a glass pane—I hate it
Invisible bubble bath, brain butt-naked
White walls bleached,
I am blanker than *nothing*

Every word I want to paint is
transparent, like lovely floral groves in arctic winter

My thoughts are see-through
My sentences, slow jogging . . .
off hidden cliffs
into
 washed-out salt canyon

Zero divided by
zero
volume in the upper cavity
"Out of order"

Lemon juice ink, the letters won't show —
the printer's broken,
it's clear
as quartz

brb.

Sometimes, I
distance myself
gently
from everyone
and everything, just
so I can take a break
and breathe
in my own world for a minute

I just need to vibe in my
quiet, little bubble for a bit, but
rest assured,
I will
always, every time,
be right back

DILUTED SUN AND MOON GOLD PAVEMENT

The shadows drip in from the west. Diluted sun and moon gold pavement stretch over his shoulders, and behind his view. The hood of an April gray sweater cuddles the musical fluids soothing his volatile sac, as well the shimmering, blue-purple
river
trickling
down
dusty brown hills.

The man lives in infinite possibilities, and unlimited other directions.

He's not here, Tonight . . . though one may see his skin and linens. He is sleeping inside a micro black-hole someplace, in hibernation. Where colors are not so saturated nor leaden, and his conscious conversations: chaotic-kind.

Life waves soft violet goodnight to its suffering soul child . . .

The weighted bags of ego and time prevail our mystery man, for now,
 for ever-changing now.

TORCHED

Black-maned crown rests slumped in pummeled wall.
Singed cables pop and silence. Sleep mode is running.
Finally.

I don't wish death, but to sleep for decades does allure.
We are an abomination.
Many tired souls in one, perpetually torn, welded
Anew by each new day unknown.

I've never wanted to hurt anyone.
Lightning strikes no hearts in a remote desert
— This haunted home was not built for public beauty.

I am a desolate machine of strange, veinish hue
Plugged into life and death, simultaneously.

Leave my body be, lest the sparks catch your eye.

The dunes of time will bury my torched house, its art and
Melancholic production.

NEGATIVE NINETY-TWO

So sensitive, uranium gremlin
Can you NOT feel everything you see?
Absorbing your photons, decibels, greedy
Let me rest with your relentless screech
Flinging sad curses; pouting in bunkered, calcium walls
Shut the fuck up.
You want to go?
Fight me already
Creepy beast peeking
Explode
You're a slimy shit

With a deep breath, I'll lightly lift your ugly

New management, same owner.
I am the property manager.
Our destiny does not hold a bitch, good sir.

I WALK IN THE LAND OF BUTS

I'm happy, but I'm slouching. Why the weird rotation, why aren't I making eye contact? *Why are you smiling? Why are you listening to me? Walk normal, breathe. They see right through you, impostor disguised ironically invisible.*

Everything is fine, but I checked my math. Changes acutely added must have a mean, multiples of differences cannot equal nothing. *Are you fucking up? Solve it, fool. Speak aloud your logged standard deviations. W0RRY W0RRY W0RRY, ye obtuse calculator of most fantastic problems!*

I'm not too broken, but rough edges cause pain. Try, though we try to change trajectory and nature, what if I am a vibrant neurotoxin, radioactive borne, slow poison—*why would you deal such a fate? You are the most pathetic destruction, all across Earth's timelines.*

Maybe, but maybe I'm not, we just needed a hug.

Everything will be just fine. But again.

DETACH

Hallway vision
Head, slip and slide, snuzzled cloud sunk
Brain dipped into shampoo bubble nap
Oxygen ocean, shoulders rock quietly
Unknown waters, time's a matter currently which
Couldn't permeate

Ambient streams carry old scents and expunged dialog

As is if asurf upon my stomach
Wisp flow drives the heavy torso on cruise
I do not exist for what were lush fourty-two seconds
The hinge clicks under my wrist

I'm sending besos for your brain.

I know the rain is feeling heavy right now
and
the water's up to your nose, but I just need you
to know that you're the most radiant person
my "old" eyes
ever laid their gaze upon. Even a blind man
can see how bright the bonfire living in your soul burns.

I want the whole world to know,
whenever I look at you, I am physically
walloped with pride and admiration.
A real love gut-check, right in my heart.
And lover of mine, if this next sentence
may persuade
even
the smallest smile
from thine lips,
consider it mine already!

While you drift and wait for the
Gray-Storm-Cloud-Metro-Express
departure, I'm sending *besos* for your brain.
Light-speed, baby.

I hope they keep the waves
in your head warm tonight.

Just until
the tide goes out, and we come
floating
down smiling, together,
and then
 . . . maybe, we get some tacos, or somethin'

SUN ROSE

The drought is over, let us all flip, out
our clothes into the desert lake, and bob our butts in joy.
The gray man is crying in color again.
Chill shivers in beat with heat, dancing a rushing swing.
Across the flowing tubes they circulate, because we are
alive, feel the flutes splash. The empty bowl has been
dusted and refilled. Misremembered the season, so I've
made it tropic spring. Cold snaps its sizzling fingers
and watches my new groove spread throughout
elegantly scarred terrain, cracking through the muddy
crust of a sun. With light and water, the flowers rose,
roses, orchids, marigolds, irises, lilies, now luff to
scented sea line. The controller belongs to the master of
this space, returned.
Shall we make this vibration infinite?

KANGAROOS SLAM UP NORTH

Sunshine
Fun days
Underwear
Underwater
Can't swim

Rolling sodium carries my head spiraled across the sea
Bleached rose gold and black float 'round fool's face
With the tepid tide rising, going, dropping
Resting me toasted on beaches increasing in brightness

Popped, scan, continue local studies

I walk the line, inhaling, smiled longer

My brain is too curious, knows he exists
Trapped behind ocean walls
Says, dropping anchors is loony
Wants to know what's outside, what more's hidden
Questions for infinity
 We're a team, I run, plut across the slipping waterfoot
 Madly
 Ironic the reason; learned so little*!*

THE ORBIT

Quiet
Finding it
Too good
Growing pains
Evolving woes
Now what
Now what
Don't want to be anybody
Just 1000 consecutive seconds
Flashbang
He's here
Everybody
All the words
 But watch this
 Oil slick rainbow
 Burn
 Recycled
 Hop on
 Breaking the sound barrier
 Losing comms
 Atmospheric, indigo, glittered streak
 First loved every soul but your own, but finally
 Burning ice
 Twist and glow
 Morph
 Louder!
 Incinerate the stone, oxygen and iron
 You are the orbit

I am the orbit

LA NIÑA NOCHE

Hi, I'm Tired.

I'm off into *la niña noche*.

I'll see you another time.

May these hours become eternity for a while.

Tomorrow's sounds aren't the slightest missed today.

Invest in my future, you two, get lost together—

rising and rolling to the final hour?

eh,

do not resuscitate before the weekend.

CHAPTER 6. NIGHT.

Alcohol, adventures, after midnight, etc.

BLACK-RABBIT HOLE

Follow me down the black-rabbit's hole
Kick the burnt
dynamite from the entrance, and
drop inside this herbaceous chute
quick
for hijinks and far-out adventures,
soulful spirits and introspection –
space-time playtime in the party dimension

We're all broken here, rid your porcelain masks!
Reveal the splintered smiles longing for oxygen
and light waves,
cosmic grooving
under
super moon, as we shed crystal tears
into neon galaxies,
together, an odd family,
until the phone-clock says
– it's time to wake up, All is here

DRUNK IN THE BATHROOM

Hey.
A potion,
fermented and potent,
hovers at your lips.
You sip it up—just a bit.
It dribbles down smooth.
Before long,
those monstrous voices inside you
subside entirely,
and you like it.

Who are you?

There's a wild-eyed man in the mirror.
He's got a familiar name
with no inhibitions.
He's leaving now,
and taking you with him.

CORRUPTED FILES

It's the latest of night here,
The stars hang and crash in the
Milky,
Confetti-black
Depths of space outside,
While the cutest
Robot-monkey,
Diminutive in the cosmos,
Rigorously decodes a possible fix for
His defective
Happy Juice machine's
Latest
 system error system error system error
system error system error system error
system error system error system error
system error system error system error

It's the latest of night here,
The stars hang and crash in the

Confetti-black

**the
Robot-monkey,**

  is defective
Happy

system error system error system error
system error system error system error
system error system error system error
system error system error system error
system error system error system error
system error system error system error
system error system error system error

system error system error system error
system error system error system error
system error system error system error
system error system error system error
system error system error system error
system error system error system error

LIQUID COURAGE

Liquid courage in my cup,
your blurry number's on my screen.
I think tonight I'll finally call you.
I hope you're not asleep.

It's chilly outside.
No snow, but I'm pretty cold.
Honestly, I'm quite intoxicated,
where I'm going, I don't really know.

In the distance behind me, I can hear the bass,
coming from a place I didn't belong.

I'm guided by this buzzed brain.
Step by step, I stumble on.

These streets I'm roaming are lamp lit mazes,
all these buildings look the same.
They converge and leave me on a hill
to gaze out upon the pulsing city veins.

I think I can see your room from here;
perhaps I'll surf the stars to your bed?
I would heed all the voices in my head,
and tell you all the things that I never said.

Above me, now, a billion suns blur,
like a spinning disco ball for gods in the sky,
and after a million miles, it seems this boozed boy's
lost track of time.

To be honest, I'm getting kind of tired.
I think I'll sit and rest.
Watch the pretty city lights dance
around my head.

Passing cars sound like **waves**
on a frosty asphalt beach.
They seem to play a lullaby
enticing me to sleep . . .

The morning mist is rolling in now,
I shiver and grip my drink tight.
Just one more sip, I'll call you.
Won't be long, tonight's the night.

UNDER THE INFLUENCE

Tonight, I'm straight cruising,
vibing away
splitting lanes in the Milky Way

12" subs are pumping
I've got my spaced-out jams bumping,
simultaneously
taking away
every last of my sad thoughts

I've got
not one clue
where my spaceship will end up
Look for the kid, though, skipping
across the stars,
bouncing his bobble head to bass and bars

Let's be honest
I might be out alien sightseeing,
but I don't quite see 20/20

Wide, *wobbly* eyes
make bright, incoming blurry
headlights
become neon streaks—
like **BILLIONS** of brilliant lasers
blazing magically across my cheeks

The wind's icy lips whistle
and kiss my face,
making me feel alive
—*DAMN, it's cold as Neptune!*

Play that next tune

Kid CuDi and J. Cole, I want you two
to take me through this astral plane
Hit that chill vibe hyperdrive
to hide my teary eyes,

and cure my astral pain

UPSIDE DOWN

What wonderful creature have I found?
She's got my head totally flipped upside down.
So beautiful but confusing
—what is she doing to me?

Care? I'm not supposed to.
My poor heart couldn't go through love's struggles,
not even once more.

My legs want to sprint from her like a
two-thousand-meter dash. My feet are fast,
I know I could run
— but her arms wrap around,
and I'm stuck to the ground.

It doesn't make sense.
How could she hold me down and

have me lifted
at the same time?

I'm supposed to be selfish, not selfless.
I keep my time locked up like
a king's collection
of precious diamonds and jewelry
—but, still,
somehow,
like magic,
 she managed to swipe it.

Surely, this must be some cruel trick
played by Cupid
dressed up looking too cute by my side.

Such a devilish, little angel,
this wonderful creature sends every
sense in my body running wild!

Why do I so badly want to run away,
yet so badly yearn for her to stay?

Alike to mini tornadoes,
she has me
hypnotized with swirling eyes,
and if I must be honest,
I quite enjoy my world the way this girl flipped it
—I'm just a little addicted, admitted.

Call me crazy, but this here fiend is sticking around.

Together, I and she will paint a piece of the universe
with our love, as we create stories of many holy nights,
and sacred late hours, when longing lips are baptized in
private and these two love drunk sinners in heat
wander
 eagerly
up carpeted
stairway steps to heaven
to worship under the retreating moon.

SNOOZE YOUR POCKET WATCH

Through the magnifying glass
— why go there?

In every dimension, are not our bodies so infinitely tiny
— why not transcend a centimeter?

Growing pills are hard to swallow with puckered lips.
Mad wisdom. You mustn't be afraid to
scramble down a rabbit hole from Time to Time.
Meet yourself microscopic. In a world of unrelentless
Waves of color, play and talk. You'll find there is nothing
new to fear
Here.

The child in that bath mirror knows the path fine.
Open your shuttered, big eyes. Breathe, and follow.

Summer sheets hold the sun and seas

Your neck smells like zero-G and shampoo
This mattress is a portal to new dimensions
On silver clouds, I am laid, open hand outstretched,
in soft fingers pressed
— the other, washed in your curves

My dreams will be dripping in your essence

The moon is blind to our bedroom, though profoundly it
glimmers in the irises locked on mine, as the celestial
tide rises and dips, rises and dips, our warm bodies and
stormy
showers in summer heat's entanglement, rocking wood
sailboat rowing moaning waves, and loud wind, aimed
for the jets of near cosmic horizon

Your legs sway fiercely, and the torrents fall

My eyes return from orbit . . . *Starry female* . . .

Worries of other hours are a dissipated hurricane

Tacos are dancing salsa in my attic.

Mischievous sizzle and salivation play on
Compact
Discs, skipping.

This cozy box, lime raindrops swarm, loudly babbling —
Precede! — there comes shortly like thunder that light
Salt
Spittle.

Drowsy thoughts: drowned in hallucinated green lava.

Let us slip to the car for a taste of reality. In stacked
Waves, thumping, the fruit water drums rise and
Pound, echoing
Round my nocturnal taste buds, nigh climax —

12:21AM

vulgar!
Closed shop. Forgive my sins.
We will share this torture.

Mischievous sizzle and salivation play on
Compact
Discs, skipping.

GPS SIGNAL LOST.

Shall we now exit the interstate, darling?
Judging by the river of red taillights
and smog,
we're not missing out on much
What say, we ditch this dreary world
and
its abundant misery?

Should My Love content, we'll split this overrated,
popsicle-melting standstill of a commute,
jumping my humble, stick-shift
planetary vehicle
through sparkly ripples in time
– bouncing to a sweet, mellow vibe across the matrix

Let the universe be our GPS,
as we swim in each other's minds,
and beaches
 on hidden worlds, just past city limits

Let us sleep each night
at peace, away or together,
soothed
by the gentle, shared light of the dimpled
moon's craters

Lorena & Whittier

Freeway exit to another world
The metal green slate atop
looms, gleams with reflective white type
Headlight beams focused, curving over
brick then foliage silhouette on sandy eve sky hanging
Curving
Curving past royal cuisine, broken paths, left to you
Black street cruise against fifty-five frames of mature
city structures, garages, booming cubic homes adjacent
Swallow up the history slinking in side-mirrors
Storing memory; each, we must
The cemetery watches, beams, *approval*, last right to
you
One last hill for the night to cook
The smallest adventure
The next taco on extended calendar stacked
Ping pong players from plate to plate
Lovers at the corner stand
Driving through our colorful kingdom
Short stories made prophecy, permanence

Keto Shakespeare

A glutton of rhymes saturated.
Wonder, maybe, I'm childish.

Diet Dr. Seuss.
I adorn my word currents and the pages drenched we go.
Not much green left for me.
Stumped by humans who destroy. Save the
art and ocean, chug my all-natural alliteration?

I'm sorry when my letters draw drooped brows.

Self conscious. The body's hat gets sick for spells.
Smiles heal untaxed.

Critics are fools.
I like to play far past Milkyway.
Because population views are broader.
I am not apt to act.
I've learned, though, the kids know.
What's life if not a space costume party?
Mix it up, millennium shakers.
Make sunken rocks flip, taste the spirit.
Bang, screw around o sea legs under
midsummer rays, white, or laser gold.
Be inspired and pleased.

I enjoy to imagine you take delight
in the collective fevered daydreams illustrated by
author.

Alas, I'm special too, if we're all?
It is possible I'm fizzle, deficient carbs.
Why art everybody run when the sidewalk is ending?

TELESCOPIC

Nike Space Hippies are dangling off of thinned sheets of hydrogen
and helium in the exosphere, space head, pointed down
to the left, inspecting the violet black void —
our gravity-woven blanket draped 'round blue corona.
Rolled my neck, counter-clockwise one hour to stare
in sad confusion. Wasted beauty.

Light-showers, blown in over cloudy dark seas,
trickle down Martian midnight hair strands onto my
eyelashes, running off the short corners of a smile to
the alien planet beneath.

Hello, Goldilocks, sixty-two thousand miles under.

I lift myself up, dance and shimmy alone on floating
space bars. Why I'm here, 'tis not for me to answer.

This place is a pool of emotions.

Cannonball.

SLEEPY

Life feels fucking good, all things considered.
I'm running on fumes, yet vivid, I feel with
the thinnest waves of static nerves
coursing through intercontinental
channels, swashing across my
muscles, enchantingly
crashing
me to
sle

CHAPTER 7. SELF-PORTRAIT.

SELF PORTRAIT-JOSHUA MUNOZ.32

Am I the man or the mirror?

Beneath the flesh and matter, be it he or I?

He only visits occasionally, but then, so does I.

Burly young chap, you look much less sad.

Life looks colorful on him lately…

Solid brusher and flosser, finally.

Talks so much without talking.

Good weird, goof smile, strangely toasty fellow.

Calculating.

Calculating.

You judge me, friend — or these eyes, yet a crude grader?

Just kidding. Look at you, Kid!

I found love!

The world's ending. We're having fun.

Thank you for reading, and welcome to my world.

However you found this book, I'm grateful for your company in this unusual space of mine.

I hope you felt. Went old places and new. I hope you saw things.

Expect my second book of poems to be published during 2025:
GOODNIGHT, BLACK HOLE. Another book of poems for infinity.

Thank you to my Mom and Dad for teaching me love and life first. Thank you for your endless sacrifices. Thank you for doing your impossibly excellent best in a wild wild world, and only time may tell how I was so unbelievably, cosmically blessed to have you as my parents. Sorry for the language. I love you.

Thank you to Angel, my brother, for continuing to remind me to seek knowledge and improvement, inside and out. Thank you for reading all my poems and giving straightforward, **critical** feedback for two decades. Thank you for trusting my words, and my deep understanding of my little brother, when I wrote you that poem to ask your high school crush out with (it wasn't meant to be). Thank you for hyping up my work so high I never doubted it. I love you.

Thank you to Andy, my brother, for brazenly being a wild card in this tasty game of life. Thank you for sparking my passion for poetry when you would praise my early work and ask for advice on your school poem projects. Thank you for not giving up and still reading my poems, even when you say they're too complicated. Thank you for always making me feel like a celebrity. I love you.

Thank you to Alaina, my sister, for never compromising your soul or spirit. Thank you for lighting up at my dreams with zero disbelief they all exist. Thank you for watching out for Mom before you should have ever needed to. Thank you for being so curious and kind about your big brother's healing trauma. Thank you for sharing pieces of your awesome world and allowing me in. I love you.

Thank you to Daniel, my brother, for showing me life can have rules that don't always need to be followed. Thank you for fanning the flame of my poetry passions when you asked me to write your middle school girlfriend a love poem (that worked, temporarily). Thank you for never stopping calling a busy brother with joy, love, and understanding when I don't write. Thank you for being so proud of me I became proud of myself. I love you.

Thank you to Marisol, my starry female, my sun girl, my sea and sun, *my Queen Taco*, for locking eyes with me on the loud dance floor. Thank you for encouraging my dreams. Thank you for reading so many poems and "final drafts". Thank you for listening to me read, excitedly. Thank you for riding rollercoasters and motorcycles with me. Thank you for unlocking honesty beside me. Thank you for trading trust, with your open heart. Thank you for shaking trees and growing love with me. I love you.

Sincerely,
Joshua Munoz
Lover Boy in Space

Thank you to Luna the Cat. The dog on the cover. She is my sol-mate's baby princess, and she brings me happiness. I love you. Cuddly, slobbery, jet-black goof catdog.

BONUS POEM:

LUNA THE CAT

Luna the Cat was a silly she-feline
Hungry and cuddly, she munched and she yawned
From sun dawn, to moon down,
Nothing but sweet nuzzles and rubs,
And
Grubbing on chow

Her fur was a sheeny, cosmic black and she barked,
For, though unaware she seemed,
Indeed, Luna was not a cat, but a dog

Made in the USA
Middletown, DE
20 November 2025